D'APRÈS TOUT
POEMS BY
JEAN FOLLAIN

THE LOCKERT LIBRARY OF POETRY IN TRANSLATION

EDITORIAL ADVISER, JOHN FREDERICK NIMS

For other titles in the Lockert Library see page 185

D'APRÈS TOUT
POEMS BY
JEAN FOLLAIN

TRANSLATED BY
HEATHER McHUGH

PRINCETON UNIVERSITY PRESS

The Lockert Library of Poetry in Translation is supported
by a bequest from Charles Lacy Lockert (1888-1974)

This book has been composed in Linotron Bodoni Book

Clothbound editions of Princeton University Press books
are printed on acid-free paper, and binding materials are
chosen for strength and durability

Printed in the United States of America by
Princeton University Press, Princeton, New Jersey

Gift

CONTENTS

ACKNOWLEDGMENTS

These translations were first featured in *The New Yorker*, *Paris Review*, and *Pequod*. The following poems, which appeared in the 6 April 1981 issue of *The New Yorker*, have been reprinted by permission: "Basically" (which appears in the present collection as "Deep Down"), "Faces," and "Event." "Cry" ("The Cry"), "Holding a Globe," "The Power of Things" ("Force of Circumstance"), "In the Morning," "Regards" ("Looks"), "Town," "The Habit" ("Habit"), "Exonerated," "Season," "People Stay on Living" ("Some People Stay"), "These Last Three Apples," and "Establishment" all appeared in volume 3, number 2 (1980) of *Pequod*, and are also reprinted by permission. Some of the final polishing was accomplished during a residency at Yaddo. The original poems were published in France by Éditions Gallimard in 1967.

I am grateful to all the people who helped me through various stages of this project, especially to Madeleine Follain, who annotated early drafts of the manuscript with tireless generosity; to Alex Fischler and Ralph Bowen, gracious consultants and readers who brought subtle sense about the poetry of it (not just the French of it) to later versions of the translation; to Jon Galassi, Bill Matthews, and Charles Simic, who gave me moral boosts over impediments to production; to Cathy Thatcher for her editing hours beyond the call of duty; and last and first to Jean Follain, *sine qua non*.

TRANSLATOR'S INTRODUCTION

Jean Follain (1903-1971) was born in Canisy, in the province of la Manche. Although he studied and practiced law in Paris, eventually to become a judge and take up permanent residence there, his poems revisit the provinces of a personal—and cultural—history ("as if representing . . . / without wishing to betray it/all of humanity"). The moments he records, by virtue of their singularity and not their generality, amount to everything. The poems are sometimes described as "miniatures," but they are not without a sense of the monumental. Indeed, it is the pressure of history upon the moment, of mortality upon the man and woman, of the unspoken (even the unspeakable) upon the poem, that makes these spare portraits so powerful.

What William Gass says of Faulkner may fairly be said (if differently meant) about Follain: "Nothing was too mean for his imagination because he did not believe there was any insignificance on earth." It is not that Follain invests humble figures with glorious language or uncommon thought but that he records their humblest gestures in such dispassionate contiguity to the movements of kings and planets. His is a generosity of attention rather than of rhetoric: faced with death, the intellectual finds for it an obscure, even an exclusive, word, while the peasant sets about eating and drinking ("Hecatomb"); a drop of water, falling, carries within it the image of a whole landscape ("Event," "Looks"); and those who can see the pasture tremble, or notice the insect scaling the mountain of a human hand, find their regard for kings and killers significantly altered ("On Thresholds"). These poems are *of moment*; the smallest detail seems crucial. Caught in the familiar gesture, in the sign of life, a human figure seems both perishable and permanent: infancy itself has its bronze footing, like the globe in "Holding a Globe"; lovers become indistinguishable from "The Statues" in the park they frequent (is it a chill in the body we feel, or a warmth in the stone?); and memory, too, is an art (the nostalgic figure in "Time of Truth" is sure "things were better arranged there"). As for the contemplative man who sits beside the statue of a woman ("Simply Waiting"), it is not only the time of day he passes, it is the time of year, the time of his life, the time of the times he lives in, already sepia in color, the weather of old photographs. In the end, he moves from the statue to the stove, he must wait so long. Follain knows that memory outlives sorrows and joys ("Animation"), even as it contains them. Each night, memory returns ("In This Light"); in each dark age the hour "has the flavor of its time" ("So Light").

If the world is read, not reduced, in the great creative acts of literature, and "on the horizon the trees/assume the outlines/of a giant sentence," then "the depth of everything increases" ("Black Meat"). So with Follain, the past and the future seem to deepen the present. Though the tense of these poems is almost always present, the sense of time is extraordinarily elastic. By making the gestures and details of medieval life, for example, so immediate in a poem about human eventuality, Follain makes time itself the subject. As readers, we recognize our three tenses in one moment and feel, for a moment, out of time. Inside the poem "Protected," the inveterate reader, whose neighbors consider him to be "short on everything" (a colloquialism felicitously suggestive of the dimensions of *their* vision), inhabits a house that, we see as we draw back (readers, ourselves) to a relativistic standpoint, is located on "a space-time curve/where a past is moving." Near the end of the poem "It's Not All Said," the swift course (cf. *"courir"* and *"court"*) of the whole human race is mentioned in passing; the words of the title are the shout of a beautiful woman in its last line. So speech identifies *us*, more than anything, as we use it; we are always its subjects.

But it is in terms of time that Follain's most subtle relativities are enacted: the convent stays as dark as it was before the reformation, while "The Real Child," without a cross to bear, "in a treeless square," whips nothing more than his spinning-top, having time only for life. And in "The Beautiful Day," the aristocratic idleness of the garden (appearing for all the world—"brushed," posed—like the subject of a more romantic art) is disturbed by the image of the insurgent mob in a living-room painting. Which is more alive, more real? We feel we know. We know we feel. Still, the man in the garden is blind.

The seer is present in these poems not as the fashionably poetic first person but rather as the subverted designer of the seen. We, the readers, have a place here too. Is it we who lull, senseless, in the garden of the decorative, blind to the blood in the living room? The poem is both subject and object here. There is a page in passage, a point in the appointed line, moment within movement. What we call "still life" the French call *"nature morte."* The present, caught in a shot, becomes something taken, or given, in a snap. *A* present is *the* present. The moment we seize is always now. When we grasp time, it feels at once to be disappearing and permanent (names we give to ink).

Throughout these poems, Follain's is the figure of the artist. "I used to like," he said of his childhood, "to crush stones down and make of them a kind of rock flour, mauve, rose, yellow. . . ." Later he would say the writer had to "relearn, to rediscover the world, finding again the naked beauty of each thing, and the affinity of simple tools for the arm of the craftsman, raised or extended." One remembers Reverdy's dictum, that the poem "*prendre sa place parmi les choses existant dans la Nature.*" These poems of *D'Après Tout* seem essential, as objects do, in just the sense Follain himself so thoroughly respected: they strike us as, simply, true.

D'APRÈS TOUT
POEMS BY
JEAN FOLLAIN

LE CRI

Dans la cité fortifiée
des quartiers s'abîment
un homme s'arrête étonné
d'une voix qui mue
une à une à l'asile
il faut laver les folles
une restant belle s'y prête
malgré des larmes silencieuses.
Des chiens s'acharnent
autour d'os à lambeaux
quelqu'un vainement crie : assez.

THE CRY

Inside the fortified city
whole blocks are falling into ruin
a man comes to a stop astonished
by a voice breaking
one by one in the asylum
the madwomen have to be washed
one still beautiful consents to it
though she weeps quietly.
Dogs are snarling over
scraps of flesh on bones
in vain somebody cries: enough.

DEVANT LES PIERRES

Cet homme qui espère
que le jour va finir
avant qu'il ne meure
pose un pied lourd
sur une première marche du perron
qu'entourent des herbes à sacrifier
les cris du groupe forcené
devant les pierres de la maison se taisent
on finit par entendre
le bruit d'une eau jaune
un caillou qui roule
la voix d'un enfant éperdu.

BEFORE THE STONES

This man who hopes
the day will end
before he dies
sets a heavy foot
on the first of the front steps
surrounded by plants that must die
the shouts of the furious mob
fall silent before the stones of the house
at last you hear
the sound of yellow water
a pebble rolling
the voice of a bewildered child.

SYMBOLES DU TEMPS

En cet univers de fuite, ils vont
hommes et femmes cheveux dans le vent
un seul reste à chanter
sous le porche d'église
on voit sur l'étendue
l'emplacement des fiefs
et restées sur la table
les cuillers d'étain
des gouttes d'eau suintent.
Les croix de pierre
de bois ou feuillage
demeurent : symboles du temps.

SYMBOLS OF TIME

Here where everything is taking flight they go
men and women the wind in their hair
only one stays to sing
under the portal of the church
the grounds of the fiefs
are visible in the distance
and left on the table
tin spoons
ooze drops of water.
Crosses of stone
of wood or leaves
remain: symbols of time.

CHOSES ET ÊTRES

Dans des faubourgs on entend
gémir des presses
tirer le vin
et même en temps de guerre.
Tout près les âcres herbes
le renard malheureux
une joueuse nue à demi
une corbeille vide
la route monotone
une question qu'on pose.

THINGS AND BEINGS

In the city's outskirts
you can hear the presses creaking
the wine flowing
even in time of war.
Right by the bitter grasses
is the miserable fox
a girl at play half-naked
an empty basket
the monotonous road
it raises a question.

DANS TOUS PAYS

Entre vie et mort
dans tous pays
il arrive qu'une fille
se déshabille pour se voir
quand elle quitte la chambre
sa beauté
laisse place au calme
parfois dans le même temps
les mains de celui qui craint sa fin
craquent dans le noir du silence
pour retenir l'espérance.

IN ALL COUNTRIES

Between life and death
in all countries
it happens that a girl
undresses to look at herself
when she leaves the room
her beauty
gives way to calm
sometimes at the same moment
the hands of the man who fears his death
crack in the black of silence
keeping a grip on hope.

TEMPS DE VÉRITÉ

Il supplie
que ne soit dévasté
ce temps de vérité
qu'il croit avoir connu
aux maisons vastes
ouvertes le jour entier.
Il assure que s'y composaient mieux
au bord de mer les algues noires
les épines-vinettes
des vives haies
les roses ouvertes.

TIME OF TRUTH

He prays
that nothing destroy
the time of truth
he thinks he has known
in spacious houses
open all day long.
He insists that things were better arranged there
on the shore the black seaweed
the barberry
quickset hedges
of roses in bloom.

SEUL HOMME

Une mouche lisse ses ailes
un pot est plein
d'allumettes éteintes
les courbes d'un verre reflètent des visages
qui couverts de cicatrices
se regardent sans s'aimer.
Sur la grande étendue
d'une campagne grise
un homme marche
comme pour représenter à lui seul
sans vouloir la trahir
toute l'humanité.

MAN ALONE

A fly polishes its wings
a jar is full
of burnt matches
the curves of a glass reflect
scar-covered faces
looking at each other without love.
On the great expanse
of a gray countryside
a man walks alone
as if representing by himself
without wishing to betray it
all of humanity.

ART DE LA GUERRE

A la fenêtre une rose a les couleurs
d'un jeune mamelon de blonde
une taupe marche sous terre.
Paix dit-on au chien
à l'existence brève.
L'air reste ensoleillé.
De jeunes hommes
apprennent à faire la guerre
pour racheter leur dit-on tout un monde
mais le livre de la théorie
leur reste illisible.

THE ART OF WAR

At the window a rose has the colors
of a blonde girl's nipple
an animal burrows underground.
Peace, someone says to the dog
whose life is short.
The air stays sunny.
Young men
are learning to make war
to redeem a whole world they are told
but the book of theory
remains illegible to them.

POURSUITE

La rouille mord
à même un fer de lance
des chevaux demeurent silencieux
cependant qu'on poursuit
un seul homme
qui court par des dédales
et des ruines
car il n'a jamais pu
s'habituer à ce temps.

PURSUIT

Rust eats
right into a spearhead
horses stand silent
as a lone man
pursued
goes running through labyrinths
and ruins
because he has never been able
to get used to his time.

TENIR UN GLOBE

L'habitant parti
la bêche usée et le râteau à dents manquantes
ne referont plus l'allée
aux empreintes de bêtes coutumières
l'enfant apporte le globe
monté sur un pied de bronze
le tourne lentement face aux collines âpres
le vent de l'automne
contourne ses mains fines
un instant il fermera les yeux
quand se soulèvera
une poussière aride
et rouge.

HOLDING A GLOBE

The inhabitant gone
the worn spade and rake with teeth missing
will never again smooth from the path
the tracks of familiar animals
the child brings out the globe
mounted on a bronze footing
turns it slowly facing the rough hills
the wind of autumn
sweeps around his delicate hands
he will close his eyes a moment
as a dry red dust is raised.

LES STATUES

Des statues d'êtres nus
à jambes longues
dans leurs postures anciennes restent souillées
parfois même on a blessé un sein
à coups de pierres ou une main
tombe dans la boue du soir
il n'y a pas eu de haine
mais tant de lèvres
ont près de socles tremblé
des fronts se sont pris
dans des mains tendres
tout d'un coup des cloches sonnent
sans qu'on sache pourquoi
une voix maussade appelle
ne se fait entendre.

THE STATUES

Statues of naked beings
with long legs
stand soiled in their ancient postures
sometimes a breast has even been wounded
by stones or a hand
falls in the evening mud
there was no hate
but so many lips
have trembled near pedestals
heads have been held
in tender hands
suddenly the bells ring
without anyone knowing why
a glum voice calls
but can't make itself heard.

VISAGES

Dans les remous des jours
des visages reviennent
l'un se détournant on aperçoit
un fin contour d'épaule
si celle que l'on regarde
est la belle aveugle
l'arbre reste tout autant soleilleux
pas de contrevents
au domaine des champs
les jours d'été y brûlent
on y sort les vieux vêtements
des mains y glissent
sur les rampes lissées
les regards s'y retrouvent
au détour brûlant
de l'allée herbue.

FACES

As the days flow together
faces come back
one of them turns away and you see
the delicate curve of a shoulder
if the one you are watching
is the beautiful blind woman
the tree stays just as full of sun
no shutters
in the kingdom of fields
here the summer days are fiery
old clothes are brought out
hands slide
on polished rails
glances meet again
here on the burning curve
of the grassy path.

SIMPLE ATTENTE

Il y a comme un reflet de lampe
sur ce visage d'homme assis
une femme nue statufiée auprès de lui.
Les jardins se défont
le coteau porte des maisons noirâtres.
Tout s'ajuste aux honneurs
après le temps d'aimer.
Il regarde la couleur sépia du temps
puis près des fourneaux
va pour attendre.

SIMPLY WAITING

There is something like lamplight reflected
on the face of this man sitting
beside a naked woman made of stone.
The gardens are overgrown
blackish houses are on the hill.
Everything takes its place for the honors
after the time of love.
He watches the sepia color of the weather
then goes by the ovens
to wait.

SUR LES SEUILS

Ceux qui inlassablement regardent
sur les seuils
sans rien faire d'autre
voient frémir l'herbage
l'attente les a durcis
apercevant ceux-là qui s'avancent
sans savoir où aller
ne regrettant pas
le règne des rois
ils ne cherchent pas à se faire meilleurs
ni à tuer
fût-ce l'insecte silencieux
qui gravit leur main.

ON THRESHOLDS

Those who tirelessly watch
on thresholds
without doing anything else
see the pasture tremble
they are used to waiting
seeing how others get ahead
without knowing where to go
they do not miss
the rule of kings
they aren't seeking to better themselves
nor to kill
even the quiet insect
climbing their hand.

SOULIER RENOUÉ

Quand le soir ébranle
sa masse de nuages
on voit le feu d'herbes
élever ses fumées
des fleurs poussent aux ravins
il reste un peu de jour
cependant qu'un garçon
à sarrau gris de fer
se penche vers l'ornière
pour renouer son soulier
sans paresse de vivre
sans trace d'absence.

TIED SHOE

When evening breaks up
its mass of clouds
the grass fire can be seen
sending up its smoke
flowers grow in the ravines
a little daylight is left
while a boy
in an iron-gray smock
bends down to the rut in the road
to tie his shoe
with no half-heartedness in life
no trace of absence.

LA PORTE

Le journalier sarcle penché
jusqu'à la nuit
il dit qu'il y a longtemps
avec un verrou à queue de porc
se fermait la porte du cellier
maintenant usée à mort,
elle geint, il l'entend.
Quel avenir, dit-il,
nous attend.
A ses pieds s'endorment
les chiens enchaînés.

THE DOOR

The day-laborer stoops over his hoe
until nightfall
he says a long time ago
the door of the cellar closed
with a bolt like a pig's tail
now used to death
it groans, he hears it.
What a future is in store for us
he says.
At his feet
the chained dogs fall asleep.

LA ROUE

Le fer passe au gris blanc
le charron pense
si disparaît la roue
je connaîtrai le vrai silence
regarderai l'ombre des tables
ne marcherai pas de travers
à force de trop boire
sentirai les forces de la terre
les mots moyeu et jantes s'oublieront
je décèlerai le vent de mer
aussi la plus fine lumière.

THE WHEEL

The iron turns gray-white
the wheelwright thinks
if the wheel disappears
I shall know true silence
I'll study the shadows of tables
won't walk crooked
from drinking too much
I'll feel the forces of the earth
the words hub and rim will be forgotten
I shall discover the ocean wind
also the subtlest of light.

MERVEILLES DU CERCLE

Quand l'orateur parle
des merveilles du cercle
on en voit s'augmenter
l'envergure du temps
les auditeurs s'animent
une femme au nom usurpé
cherche à comprendre
avec de grands yeux noirs
des rides profondes au front.
Pour chacun bientôt les couleurs changent.

WONDERS OF THE CIRCLE

When the orator speaks
of the wonders of the circle
the span of time
appears to enlarge
listeners grow animated
a woman with an assumed name
is trying to understand
with great dark eyes
deep wrinkles in her brow.
Soon for everyone the colors change.

CERCEAUX

Des femmes à cheveux longs
ont orné ces enfants
dont courent les cerceaux
sur la route durcie
une première étoile
se montre au jardin.
La paix s'étend sur ces communes
où l'on aime à regarder les astres
pour durer
deviner.

HOOPS

Long-haired women
have adorned these children
whose hoops are rolling
on the hardened road
a first star
can be seen in the garden.
Peace spreads over these villages
where one loves to look at stars
in order to survive
to foretell.

LES INCENDIAIRES

Le vieil incendiaire a rencontré le jeune
ils se voient dans les glaces
des magasins déchus
ils perdent leur mémoire
un tas de tessons
jette des lueurs vivaces
pas une feuille à l'arbre
n'est pareille à l'autre
toutes ensemble tremblent
pour exister.

THE INCENDIARIES

The old incendiary has met the young one
they see themselves in the mirrors
of ruined stores
they are losing their memory
a heap of shards
throws off lively gleams
not a leaf on the tree
is like another
all together tremble
to exist.

AFFRONTER L'ANIMAL

N'est pas toujours facile
d'affronter l'animal
même s'il vous regarde sans trouble ni haine
il le fait fixement
et semble dédaigner
le fin secret qu'il porte
paraît mieux sentir
l'évidence du monde
celle qui jours et nuits
taraude et blesse à l'âme
dans le bruit, le silence.

FACE THE ANIMAL

It's not always easy
to face the animal
even if it looks at you
without fear or hate
it does so fixedly
and seems to disdain
the subtle secret it carries
it seems better to feel
the obviousness of the world
that noisily day and night
drills and damages
the silence of the soul.

MARÉE

Des couleurs de poissons
s'estompent aux matins blancs
parfois sonne aussi
la corne du vendeur avec le glas
les chiens de mer sont contemplés
par des hommes affables
cherchant une douceur.
Qui veut s'en revenir
par les chemins d'hier
clame un fils de veuve
en humant cette odeur
de goémons noirs
qui traverse l'espace
sur la terre et la mer.

TIDE

Colors of fish
fade on white mornings
sometimes too the vendor's horn
sounds as the death knell does
dogfish are examined
by affable men
looking for a delicacy.
Who wants to escape
down the roads of the past
shouts the widow's son
inhaling that smell
of black seaweed
which crosses the space
on earth and sea.

L'INSECTE NOIR

Sur la pierre noire
selon un proverbe arabe
Dieu voit aller l'insecte noir
qui même poursuivant sa route sur du blanc
se perd au regard
d'homme au cœur saignant
qui contemple
les lignes de ses mains
mais quand ses yeux
se posent sur la route
il ne reconnaît plus
quand elle y passe
la femme qui l'aima.

THE BLACK INSECT

On the black stone
says an Arab proverb
God sees the black insect move
which even going its way on white
is lost to the eye
of the man with a bleeding heart
who contemplates
the lines in his hands
but when his eyes
settle on the road
he no longer recognizes
the woman who loved him
as she walks by.

LE LIERRE

Un blanc lierre mort
concrétion sur le mur
sous les nuées s'étire.
Parmi les hommes arrêtés
au plus âgé le soir à venir
paraît moins loin
il caresse un pelage
dont il s'émeut
en ville éperdument
dans la grande rue large
alors sans personne
bat l'enseigne usée
au milieu des soupirs.

IVY

A dead white ivy
is concrete on the wall
far-reaching under clouds.
Among the men who pause there
the evening to come
seems less distant
to the oldest
he strokes an animal's fur
which stirs his emotions
in town in desperation
in the broad main street
with no one around
the worn-out sign swings
back and forth in sighs.

BLESSURES

Une plante de muraille se déchire
sous le coup de caillou
d'un sournois vigilant
une femme laisse tomber
un linge
d'une main moite
s'endort la gorge blessée
le vent secoue une balançoire
pourrissante
un mot revient à la surface
pour repartir dans l'oubli
des vapeurs montent de la terre abritée.

WOUNDS

A plant growing out of a wall
is ripped by the impact of the stone
thrown by a sharp-eyed prowler
a woman lets a cloth fall
from her damp hand
loses consciousness
wounded in the breast
the wind stirs
a rotting swing
a word comes to mind
then sinks into forgetfulness again
vapors rise from the protected earth.

TISANE

Il s'en trouve à prétendre
qu'une tisane de jusquiame
fait voir les démons
une femme va en boire
cheveux déployés
un peu de fine terre
entre ses orteils nus
ne l'attend personne
le breuvage à couleur rouille
remplit un bol fileté bleu.

INFUSION

There are those who say
that a broth of henbane
makes you see demons
a woman is about to drink some
her hair undone
a little fine soil
between her bare toes
no one is waiting for her
the brew the color of rust
fills a bowl with veins of blue.

ÉTABLISSEMENT

Dans une venelle
un établissement porte en enseigne
le seul mot café en lettres noires.
Quelqu'un y assure :
mon père assis sur une chaise
parle du démon rouge
que terrasse l'archange.
Un bijou à facettes reste
sur sa console.
Il sait prendre la vie.

ESTABLISHMENT

In an alleyway
an establishment bears by way of sign
the one word café in black letters.
Someone here is laying down the law:
my father sitting in a chair
tells how the archangel
cast the scarlet devil down.
A cut gem rests
on his sideboard.
He knows how to live.

PROTÉGÉ

Plein d'affabulations
il nourrit chez lui
un rat invincible
pour qu'il ne dévore pas ses livres.
Dans son voisinage ils déclarent
ce n'est pas raisonnable
il manque de tout.
Lui écoute la pluie éclatante
ou faible
protégé par des murs noircis
une lande, les buissons
sur une courbe d'espace et de temps
où un passé bouge.

PROTECTED

Full of strange notions
he feeds an invincible rat in his house
to keep it from eating his books.
In his neighborhood they declare
it's not reasonable
he's short on everything.
As for him, he listens to the rain
loud or light
protected by blackened walls
the barrens, the bushes
on a space-time curve
where a past is moving.

TOUT N'EST PAS DIT

Dans ce lieu pur
du soir au matin vont
des bêtes sans pensée
les arbres tremblent
stagne un étang à reflets
les déserts poursuivent leurs mirages.
Passent ceux de la race humaine.
Tout n'est pas dit clame
la plus belle.

IT'S NOT ALL SAID

From evening to morning
in this virgin place
animals come and go
without thinking
the trees tremble
the reflecting pool stagnates
deserts pursue their mirages.
Those of the human race go by.
It's not all said
shouts the most beautiful woman.

LE PACTE

Les lumières soufflées
les tenailles posées sur l'établi
le temps passe.
Résistent aussi l'aire en terre battue
les chaumes.
Écrit à l'encre bourbeuse
frappé de cire noire
le pacte conclu entre puissances
demeure lourd de menaces.
L'enfant pauvre joue avec la boue
le riche avec le sable.
Une tristesse se répand
dans des salles sans écho.

THE PACT

The lamps blown out
pincers placed on the workbench
time passes.
Thatched roofs
and the floor of beaten earth survive.
Written in muddy ink
sealed with black wax
the pact between powers
remains heavy with menace.
The poor child plays with mud
the rich with sand.
A sadness spreads
through rooms with no echo.

FORCE DES CHOSES

Croyant entendre frapper
on prend la lampe on ouvre la porte
pour ne trouver que le vent
ce n'est pas le vieil infirme
ni la bête effarée
qui frôlante et tremblante
jouit pourtant d'exister
toutes les fenêtres sont bien fermées.
Beaucoup
refusent le souvenir
mais l'oubli n'est complet jamais.

FORCE OF CIRCUMSTANCE

Thinking you hear knocking
you take the lamp open the door
to find nothing but wind
it's not the old cripple
not the frightened beast
which trembling and brushing past
nevertheless likes being alive
all the windows are shut tight.
Many
refuse to remember
but forgetfulness is never complete.

HÉCATOMBE

Le ciel reste bleu intense
quand plusieurs tombent morts
le vieux penseur
qui ne veut pas changer le langage
ne trouve pour pareil fait
qu'un seul mot : hécatombe.
Les paysans qui survivent
dans le plein soleil
se mettent à boire
et manger sobrement.

HECATOMB

The sky stays intense blue
when several people drop dead
the old thinker
who doesn't want to change the language
can find for such a fact
but one word: hecatomb.
The farmers who survive
in broad daylight
begin soberly
to eat and drink.

LA FÊTE DES CHIENS

Dans un pays d'Asie
un jour l'an on fête les chiens
ils portent alors des guirlandes de fleurs
leur front est marqué de poudre rouge
ils hument l'air
regardent comme hier les stratus de ciel
l'un comme les autres orné
tremble et va mourir
sans rien savoir.

FESTIVAL OF DOGS

In an Asian country
one day a year the dogs are honored
they wear garlands of flowers
their faces are marked with red powder
they sniff the air
look at the clouds in the sky
as they did yesterday
one decked out like the others
trembles and goes off to die
none the wiser.

PAR LES CHAMPS

Ces champs à vives haies
ils les voient tous les jours
dans l'approximation du temps
sur une bascule énorme et fissurée
ils pèsent sans pouvoir connaître
le nombre des épis
qu'agite une brise
des femmes se montrent aux lumières
un grand mur nu s'allonge
parfois intervient
un léger baiser sur les lèvres.

THROUGH THE FIELDS

Every day they see these fields
of quickset hedges
on a great cracked scale
in the approximation of the time
they weigh without being able to know
the number of grains
a breeze stirs
women appear in shifts of light
a high bare wall stretches out
sometimes someone gets
a light kiss on the lips.

INTÉRIEUR HABITÉ

Des taches sur le mur
voisinent celles du pelage
d'une bête alarmée
un homme vient de loin
une petite main s'enferme
dans une grande fissurée
un souffle fait disparaître
l'insecte à jamais
un nom reste pâli
sur une porte à moulures
un bois d'escalier geint
les deux bras s'ouvrent
d'une beauté épanouie.

INHABITED INTERIOR

Spots on the wall
resemble those on the coat
of a frightened animal
a man is coming from far off
a small hand is clasped
in a large rough one
a breath makes the insect
disappear forever
a faded name remains
on a doorway with moldings
the wood of a staircase creaks
a radiant beauty
opens both arms wide.

FACE AUX OSIERS

Elle ne défait que nue
l'ordre des tresses
face aux osiers du lourd jardin
la peau mate dans l'ombre
la chandelle morte dans le cuivre
longtemps encore elle aura
du cœur à l'ouvrage
de l'émoi aux seins
avec l'image
dans la ville à remparts
des marchands en plein vent.

FACING THE WILLOWS

Only naked does she undo
the arrangements of her hair
facing the willows of the heavy garden
her skin dull in the shade
the candle dead in the brass holder
for a long time to come she will have
heart in her work
feeling in her breasts
at the memory
of open-air merchants
in the walled town.

LA RECHERCHE

Le verre à pied se brise
dans ce jour vulnérable
plein d'enchevêtrements
et sans guère de paroles
sous une armoire sombre
une fille cherche un chausson
on entend respirer
son corps lisse
aux vêtements déteints à reprises légères
parfois toute la maison tressaille
qui prend assise
au bord d'un abîme.

THE SEARCH

The stemmed glass breaks
on this vulnerable day
full of mixed feelings
and with scarcely a word
a girl looks under a dark cupboard
for her slipper
you can hear
her smooth body breathing
in fading delicately mended clothes
sometimes the whole house shudders
coming to rest
on the edge of an abyss.

TRAVAUX

Les travaux à la brume
se continuent
du tisserand de la brodeuse.
Un bol brun reste
sur la table à long profil
qu'aborde un insecte rouge.
La beauté sculptée lentement
se tient avivée par le froid
dans un atelier géant
qui domine un précipice à végétaux immortels.

WORK

Work goes on in the dim light:
the work of the weaver
and of the woman who embroiders.
A brown bowl sits
on the table whose long edge
a red insect is climbing.
The beauty slowly being sculpted
is kept alive by cold
in a giant workshop
atop a cliff of everlasting plants.

EXONÉRÉ

Il quitte les lieux l'exonéré
de tout lien
avec un bâton noueux
tout écœuré d'odeurs
d'abord il reste muet
passant devant les rocs
peut-être veut-il se rendre
dans un pays moins beau.
Que personne ne rie
crie-t-il au pied des monts.
Un écho répète
l'insolite injonction multipliée.

EXONERATED

The man freed from all ties
leaves the premises
with a gnarled walking stick
utterly sick of smells
at first he keeps silent
walking past the faces of rock
maybe he'd rather move
to a less beautiful place.
Let no one laugh
he cries at the foot of the mountains.
An echo repeats
and multiplies the odd command.

FEMME ENTOURÉE

Tiennent le peuple en haleine
ces remous autour d'une femme
qui reste belle
quand elle courbe son corps
ses cheveux balayant un sol rouge
dans l'ultime lumière de fête.
Tous ceux-là qui regardent
se souviennent
mais ne voient plus
s'avancer la nuit.

SURROUNDED WOMAN

People are kept in suspense
by these commotions about a woman
who remains beautiful
as she bends her body
her hair sweeping the red ground
in the last light of festivities.
All those who watch
have memories
but they no longer see
night approaching.

FACE A SON PASSÉ

L'un précise qu'à la guerre
son ami sous l'obus
derrière lui
se réduisit en déchiquetures
qui tombèrent sur son dos
l'eau du fleuve
n'emprunte plus l'image du soldat mort.
Là où luit un vague soleil
quand des nuages marchent sans fin
pour prendre de l'avance
sur la longue durée
face à son passé
on reste.

FACING HIS PAST

One man explains that in the war
his friend under shelling
behind him
was reduced to shreds
that fell on his back
the water of the river
no longer gives back the image of the dead soldier.
There where a dim sun gleams
as clouds march endlessly on
in order to get ahead
in the long run
a man stays
facing his past.

ÉQUIVOQUE

Équivoque de retrouver belles
des choses
usées et muettes
une pierre est là
dure et veinée
la poésie quelqu'un dit
qu'il n'en veut plus
l'on perçoit l'éclat d'un rire
un sanglot sous les futaies
la pluie détériore
les maisons jusqu'aux horizons
on entend marcher
derrière un mur sans rien savoir.

EQUIVOCATION

It is equivocation to find
worn wordless things
beautiful again
a stone is there
hard and veined
poetry someone says
he wants no more of it
the burst of a laugh is heard
a sobbing under the trees
the rain wears down the houses
all the way to the horizon
he hears footsteps
behind a wall without knowing anything.

L'ENFANT RÉEL

Le ciel se couvre
dans un couvent près de bêtes sculptées
des religieuses passent
qui semblent par l'ombre gantées et masquées
comme avant le temps des réformes
mais en plein bourg soleilleux
sur une place sans arbres
fouettant par devoir
sa toupie de buis
un enfant reste bien réel
sans temps morts.

THE REAL CHILD

The sky grows overcast
in a convent near sculptures of animals
nuns come and go
looking masked and gloved by shade
as before the time of reforms
but in the sunlit middle of town
in a treeless square
practicing the whiplash
on his hardwood spinning-top
a child stays very real
without killing time.

ÉPOQUES

Que de main-d'œuvre
dans ces tressaillants rideaux
figurant des dieux
certains bourgeois acclamèrent
d'autres se terrèrent
entre des murs nus
un corps parfois s'offre
dans ces époques troublées
s'il y survit
il se peut qu'il ouvre la porte
donnant sur une cour glacée
où gît un mannequin
aux yeux bleus
couvert de terre argileuse.

TIMES

What handiwork
in these fluttering curtains
depicting the gods
certain citizens cheered
others hid themselves
between bare walls
sometimes a body presents itself
in these troubled times
if it survives
it may open the door
onto a frozen courtyard
where a blue-eyed mannequin lies
covered with clay.

ENCRIER SOLITAIRE

Il est un champignon dénommé
encrier solitaire
aussi œuf noir
il reste sans autres autour de lui
s'en approchent des bêtes blanches
la haie apparaît en feu
le cœur d'une femme qui passe
bat fort en elle
elle revoit si loin
les vagues d'océan
elle traverse le pont étroit
alors les maisons du faubourg
apportent des rayons de lumière.

SOLITARY INKWELL

There is a mushroom called
solitary inkwell
also black egg
it stands with no others about it
white animals come close
the hedge appears to be on fire
the heart of a woman who passes by
beats hard within her
she is seeing so far off again
the ocean waves
she crosses the narrow bridge
and then the houses of the outskirts
shed some rays of light.

ÉVÉNEMENT

Tout fait événement
pour qui sait frémir
la goutte qui tombe
portant les reflets
de granges et d'étables
le son d'une épingle
tombant sur un marbre
le lait qui bout
à la fin des jours
les moments qui traînent
en de pâles séjours
quand s'endort la femme.

EVENT

Everything is an event
for those who know how to tremble
the droplet that falls
carrying reflections
of barns and stables
the sound of a pin
falling on marble
milk boiling
at day's end
the moments that drag
in colorless rooms
when the woman falls asleep.

D'AVENTURE

Survient l'aventure
au milieu du bruit
d'enfants condamnés
à toujours jouer
le temps ne reviendra pas
que l'on mélangeait au vin rouge
la suie aux reflets d'argent
pour en faire une encre rurale
entrer dans la pièce en sortir
beaucoup s'y feront
se retrouvant seuls toujours
un soir tout se termine
que fenêtres closes sur un jardin
à fleurs rouges
passent les heures
creuses de la nuit.

BY CHANCE

The chance presents itself
in the midst of the noise
of children condemned
forever to play
the time won't come again
when silver-flecked soot
was mixed with red wine
to make a rural ink
many people will get used to
entering a room, leaving it
finding themselves always alone
everything stops one evening
when windows shut on a garden
of red flowers
the hollow hours
of the night go by.

FAUSSE CROISADE

Une femme longuement parfumée
farde une bouche amère
attache des jarretelles usées
par un midi de vaste azur
passent ceux-là déguisés en croisés
montés pour la cavalcade
sur des chevaux de labour
ils comblent les espaces étroits du village
aperçoivent un futur dérisoire
mais malgré tout l'espoir.

MOCK CRUSADE

A carefully perfumed woman
puts make-up on her bitter mouth
attaches worn garters
in a noonday of vast blue
those disguised as crusaders go by
mounted for the cavalcade
on plowhorses
filling the narrow spaces of the town
they see derision in the future
but in spite of everything, hope.

ARRÊT D'HORLOGE

Des bêtes restent sans effroi
de leur mort prochaine
vêtu de noir un homme rêve
aux seins d'une femme pauvre
alors que se refroidit
la pulpe des fleurs
devant des palissades
battues par les vents.
Longtemps le silence a duré
l'horloge au coffre de bois
sonne pleinement
puis ses aiguilles s'arrêtent
dans la chambre des victimes.

STOPPED CLOCK

Some animals never feel dread
of their approaching death
dressed in black a man dreams
of a poor woman's breasts
while along the fences
battered by wind
the flesh of flowers
grows cold.
Silence has lasted a long time
the clock in its wooden case
strikes the hour
then its hands stop
in the victims' room.

AU FOND

Sans faire un grand pas
au fond pense un homme
je suis peut-être heureux
près de moi un oiseau
sans chanter bat de l'aile
l'ombre se rapprochant
la femme se tait
mais dans son rêve parle
sur la fauve étendue
bruissent des branches
résonnent des pas
le couteau jeté dans la fureur
rouille auprès d'un hêtre
quand finiront les guerres
interroge un passant
léger aux cheveux blancs
depuis beau temps déjà
on ne répond pas.

DEEP DOWN

Without making any big step
a man thinks deep down
maybe I am happy
a bird nearby
flutters without singing
darkness coming on
the woman falls silent
but speaks in her dream
on the tawny expanse
branches rustle
footsteps echo
the knife thrown in anger
rusts by a beech tree
when will wars be over
a passerby asks
wispy with white hair
it's a good long time
since anyone answered.

DES GENS DEMEURENT

Qu'il fasse gris, noir ou rouge
des gens demeurent
ouvrent des barrières usées
hors d'eux-mêmes
attendent qu'on les vienne surprendre
un soir ou l'autre
pour les sortir du lieu de refuge
ils voient la même étoile que d'autres
mais aussi par terre une boîte éventrée
où rien ne reste.

SOME PEOPLE STAY

Whether it is gray, black or red outside
some people stay
they open the worn gates
beside themselves
waiting to be surprised
one evening or another
to be taken from their place of refuge
they see the same star as others
but also on the ground a gutted box
with nothing left inside.

LA HAINE

D'abord
la croûte du pain impose le calme
le troupeau passe
sans peur et vif
un tremblement saisit
un arbuste presque mort
puis la haine éclate
dans une chaumière
et l'homme est écarlate.

HATE

At first
a crust of bread imposes peace
the herd goes by
lively and unafraid
a trembling seizes
a nearly dead bush
then hate breaks out
in a cottage
and the man is scarlet.

LARRON

Le cœur des vaches bat dans le pré
un homme y vient voler leur lait
marchant dans la fraîcheur de la rosée
il n'aime ni ne hait
pour lui seul s'arrête le temps
le soleil arrivé haut dans le ciel
alors il ne peut que dormir
répudiant
enfance, âge adulte, vieillesse.
S'il passe rien ne sert de crier :
Attendez.

THIEF

The cows' hearts beat in the meadow
a man is coming to steal their milk
walking in the coolness of the dew
he neither loves nor hates
for him alone time stops
the sun high in the sky
then he can do nothing but sleep
repudiating
childhood, adulthood, old age.
If he passes, it's no use to cry:
Wait.

LA MER

Qui paie à boire
clame un marin
à d'autres qui regardent la mer
accotés aux murs cimentés
tandis que passent bonnes et mauvaises femmes
devant les filets enflammés
par la grande lumière étrange.

THE SEA

Who's paying for drinks
shouts a sailor
to others who look at the sea
leaning on cemented walls
while good and bad women go by
the nets aflame
in the great strange light.

LE PASSANT DE L'AUBE

Cette maison avec toute l'existence devant soi
la contourne
le passant de l'aube
qui tient dans sa main
la laisse au mousqueton rouillé
d'un chien jaune et muet
la prudence dicte le silence
tant de choses se passent
à l'intérieur des chambres.
Comment rentrer
dans les rêves de la vie?

PASSERBY AT DAWN

Around this house with all of life before it
the passerby walks at dawn
holding in his hand
the quiet yellow dog's
leash with the rusty snap
prudence dictates silence
so many things go on
inside of bedrooms.
How to get back
into the dreams of life?

UNE AURORE

En une ville grisaille
un ciel de lit tombe sur des corps endormis
qui réveillés en rient.
Bientôt se montrent des lueurs d'aurore
des voix se répondent
d'une maison à jardin à une autre.
On entend sans arrêt
l'aboi du chien
le monde ne s'en défait pas moins
pour ces hommes à front têtu
qui attendent sans parler
fixent l'espace.
Enfants ils jouèrent.

ONE SUNRISE

In a charcoal-gray town
the canopy of a bed falls on sleeping bodies
who wake up laughing about it.
Soon the glimmers of sunrise appear
voices call back and forth
from one garden-house to another.
You can hear the ceaseless
baying of a dog
the world falls apart no less
for those men with stubborn brows
who wait without speaking
and stare into space.
They played games when they were children.

AU MATIN

Voici les marcheurs
à pèlerines noirâtres
aux blouses qui s'usent
les herbes flottantes
les poissons sanglants
que revend un marchand revêtu de haillons
dans un monde captif d'écoliers et de maîtres.
Une glace reste brisée
une porte va s'ouvrir
un courant d'air vibrant
peut faire mourir.

IN THE MORNING

Here are the people out walking
in blackish capes
and worn-out blouses
the grasses afloat
the bloody fish
sold by a dealer dressed in rags
in a captive world of schoolchildren and teachers.
A mirror lies shattered
a door is about to open
a bracing draft of air
could kill you.

PRÈS DU MÊME ARBRE

Le maître défendait
que même las
on s'étendît dans la journée
souvent les mots
lui restaient sur les lèvres
au fond du jardin
plein de guêpes et de ronces
il restait parfois près du même arbre
debout et la main sur l'écorce
le chien pouvait seul
se coucher à ses larges pieds.

BY THE SAME TREE

The teacher forbade
that even when weary
one should lie down during the day
often the words
never left his lips
at the far end of the garden
full of wasps and thorns
he remained sometimes by the same tree
upright with his hand on the trunk
only the dog
could lie at his large feet.

REGARDS

Un malade fixe
d'un long regard
une goutte d'eau
portant le reflet
d'un fin paysage.
Une tache de vin
en forme de France
reste à son visage.
La mousse d'un cidre amer
s'apaise sur la table brune
toujours un lait bout
quelque peu avant
que la nuit ne vienne
en ce lieu du monde
où des yeux voient
un instant loin.

LOOKS

A sick man looks
a long time
at a drop of water
carrying the reflection
of a tiny landscape.
A red birthmark
in the shape of France
is left on his face.
On the brown table the foam
of the fermented cider goes flat
milk is still boiling
a little before night comes
in this part of the world
where for a moment
eyes see far away.

PRIS DANS LE PAYSAGE

Pris dans le paysage à désirs humains
ils passent ensemble
devant l'ancienne filature
hagarde et sans carreaux
seule la femme soupire
parfois s'interpose
une fête civique
de longs nuages fuient sur le ciel
un bras dessine une ligne pure
ignorantes du temps
les bêtes domestiques connaissent leur chemin
et le suivent.

CAUGHT IN THE LANDSCAPE

Caught in the landscape of human desires
they go together
past the abandoned spinning mill
wild and windowless
only the woman sighs
sometimes a civic celebration
comes between them
long clouds flee across the sky
an arm sketches a perfect line
ignorant of time
the domestic animals know their path
and follow it.

REPAS

Dans l'assiette blanche
un peu ébréchée
on mange un morceau de viande saignante
la femme assoiffante
on ne la voit plus.
Sur la route bleue
puis qui devient rouge
de grands chiens passent
comme s'ils avaient
moyen d'exister
durant tous les temps
en portant collier à plaque de cuivre
au nom de leur maître
et sans peur de la nuit.

MEAL

From the slightly chipped
white plate
you eat a piece of rare meat
you no longer see
the woman you thirst for.
On the blue road
which then becomes red
large dogs go by
as if they had
a way of surviving
to the end of time
by wearing collars with brass tags
in the name of their master
and not being afraid of the dark.

RETOUR OU PAS

Des marchepieds de bois veiné
aident pour monter dans de hauts lits
couleur de litharge.
Un champignon pousse en une nuit.
Ceux-là qui partent
reviendront-ils vivants
avec la rage au corps
ou dans la paix précaire
d'un jour élargi
qui toujours s'achève?

RETURN OR NOT

Footstools of grained wood
help you climb into high beds
the color of oxidized lead.
A mushroom comes up in a night.
Will those who leave
come back alive
their bodies full of passion
or in the precarious calm
of a day at large
that always comes to an end?

SAISON

Près des souches de chêne
sont les marques de pas
d'un robuste fuyard
sous le ciel de jadis
la châtaigne éclate
sous la cendre d'hiver
les métamorphoses
épuisent les jardins
voir le pain fait rire
l'enfant des misérables
mais celui des riches
sourit à l'arc-en-ciel
sa mère en robe mauve
le tenant par la main
ils marchent tous les deux
vers l'horizon qui s'ouvre.

SEASON

By the oak tree stumps
are the footprints
of a robust runaway
under the sky of long ago
the chestnut bursts open
under the ashes of winter
metamorphoses
exhaust the gardens
the sight of bread
makes the pauper's child laugh
but the child of the wealthy
smiles at the rainbow
his mother in a mauve dress
taking him by the hand
they walk together
out into the open.

ANIMATION

Un travesti brûlant
la moulait au plus juste
l'ouragan sans raison
remuait les cieux
déchirant des fleurs
courbant l'herbe noire
cette femme sous sa peau
épiait son sang
le temps dérivant
sur les bois et plaines
partout se frayaient leurs voies
douleurs et joies
au jour à l'autre attentives
mais survivant à toutes
une mémoire active.

ANIMATION

A burning disguise
clung to her closely
without reason the hurricane
stirred the heavens
shredding flowers
bending the black grass
like a spy this woman
watched the blood
under her skin
the weather drifting
over woods and plains.
Everywhere sorrows and joys
made their path
looking after one day at a time
but an active memory
outlived them all.

CULTIVATEURS

Des cultivateurs restent
devant les nuages
dont ils cherchent le sens
d'aucuns au silence
préfèrent l'emphase habile
au coin d'une haie
à multiples plantes
des soirs transparents
se répètent et s'usent
sur des tréteaux
on parle aux attablés
dans la grange ouverte
sur des labours illuminés
au fin bout du monde.

FARMERS

Some farmers keep on
watching the clouds
looking for clues
some prefer
an easy eloquence
to silence
at the corner
made by a hedge
of many plants
the transparent evenings
wear thin with repetition
on a stage of trestles
someone is making a speech
to others seated at tables
in the open barn
on furrows that shine
to the very ends of the earth.

PAR CE JOUR

Pleinement
par ce grand jour on voit
le bol vide sur la table
au fond un miroitement avec le jeu des ombres
parmi les passants
l'un ramasse une épingle
sous un ciel qui s'assombrit
sans que les lampes s'allument.
Un corps suave
se pénètre du silence.
Des images de la mémoire
reviendront avec le soir.

IN THIS LIGHT

Clearly in this broad daylight you can see
the empty bowl on the table
the background dappled
with the play of shadows
among the passersby
one picks up a pin
under a sky that darkens
though no lights come on.
A lithe body
is filled with silence.
Images from memory
will return with evening.

LA BELLE JOURNÉE

Insectes et poissons
passent de l'ombre à la lumière
les fruits tiennent encore à l'arbre
frôlés par l'aile affinée
d'un oiseau flamboyant
puis d'un autre mat.
A ses yeux disparus
l'aveugle pense à peine
dans le jardin à fleurs rouge vineux.
D'un coup dans le salon le soleil éclaire
un grand tableau qui figure
une survenue effarante d'émeutiers.

THE BEAUTIFUL DAY

Insects and fish
move from the shade to the light
the fruit hangs still on the tree
brushed by the fine wing
of a flamboyant bird
then a dull one.
The blind man hardly thinks
of his missing eyes
in the garden of wine-red flowers.
Suddenly the sun in the drawing room
lights a large painting that shows
rioters surging wildly into sight.

SEULE JOURNÉE

Dans un prétoire au vieux bois
un homme dit :
quand j'ai peur j'invente une image
un carrosse dédoré
aux chevaux peinant
gravit une route gelée
on demande à l'enfant son âge
la journée n'en est pas perturbée
le miracle ne se produira pas
la nuit survient vite
toutes portes se ferment
sur le monde hivernal
des enfances exténuées.

A SINGLE DAY

In an old wood-panelled courtroom
a man says:
when I'm afraid I imagine a scene
its gilt gone, a coach
with straining horses
climbs an icy road
the child is asked his age
the day is undisturbed by this
no miracle will happen
night comes quickly
all doors close
on the winter world
of children's worn-out lives.

A L'ÉCOUTE

La vision demeure
tremble la main qui la transcrit
dans la salle d'auberge étoilée.
Le soir submerge
le champ de pommes de terre.
Quand le cultivateur entend les pas sur le chemin
il s'arrête de fouir
puis se prend à écouter
pour son seul usage
les bruits de son monde.

LISTENING

The vision persists
the hand that transcribes it trembles
in a starlit room at the inn.
Evening submerges
the potato field.
When the farmer hears the steps on the path
he stops digging
then starts to listen
to the sounds of his world
for his own use.

UN CRÉPUSCULE

La presse à bras ne sert plus
que tachent des encres durcies
les chambres à gaz s'éteignent
l'ombre d'une main effilée
se montrera précise
sur un mur sanglant
des fronts se rejoindront
les oiseaux se tairont
et par le sentier
des enfants porteront pour leur dîner
une écuellée
de haricots blancs dans leur sauce figés.

TWILIGHT

The handpress is no longer used
stained with hardened ink
the gas chambers are extinguished
the shadow of a thin hand
will show up clearly
against a bloody wall
faces will meet again
the birds will fall silent
and along the path
children will carry for supper
a bowlful
of white beans congealed in their sauce.

ALLUMEZ DONC

Les œillets du corset
jettent leurs reflets
des persiennes fermées
protègent un monde
dont l'illusion
s'effondrera.
L'heure a le goût de son temps.
Allumez donc les lampes
entend-t-on, voyons
c'est la nuit.

SO LIGHT

The eyelets of the corset
cast reflections
closed venetian blinds
protect a world
the illusion of which
will dissolve.
The hour has the flavor of its time.
So light the lamps
someone says, see here
it's night.

LA CONSTANCE

Des vêtements tombent un à un
en pleine paix se dénude un corps
dehors les maisons
les étables s'allument
dorment encore
les travailleurs de nuit
une femme fera un songe sans issue
un homme à visage d'enfant
poussera une voiture à bras
pleine de livrées
à dorures enlevées.

CONSTANCY

Articles of clothing fall one by one
in complete peace a body gets undressed
outside the houses
lights are coming on in the stables
the nightworkers
are still sleeping
a woman will have a dream with no outcome
a man with a child's face
will be pushing a handcart
full of uniforms
their gold trim removed.

VIANDE NOIRE

Autour de pierres précieuses
qu'usent seulement
leur propre poussière
des mangeurs coupent
leur viande noire
à l'horizon les arbres
imitent dans leurs contours
une phrase géante
les images se transforment
avec les fuites de lumière
on entend mâcher
la venaison.
De tout la profondeur augmente.

BLACK MEAT

Near precious stones
that are worn down only
by their own dust
eaters are cutting
their black meat
on the horizon the trees
assume the outlines
of a giant sentence
images are transformed
with shifts of light
you can hear the venison
being ground by teeth.
The depth of everything increases.

PARCIMONIEUSE ÉCOLE

A la parcimonieuse école
on n'apprend pas
les danses amoureuses des pieuvres
mais à lire épître évangile
le boucher éventrant ses bœufs
n'y fut jamais.
Du fond du cachot
la cloche à l'oreille sonne.
Époque des nuages de gloire
de la grâce.

SCHOOL OF PARSIMONY

In the school of parsimony
they don't learn
the love dances of the octopus
but to read epistle and gospel
the butcher disembowelling his oxen
never went there.
From the depth of a dungeon
a bell rings in the ear.
Era of clouds of glory
and grace.

SÉPARATION

Dans un hangar du vieux jardin
la séparation s'accomplit
aux bruissements des feuillages
il faut s'éloigner
pour un autre pays
pour retrouver ce moment d'adieu
accoté à l'arbre calme
dans l'heure des lampes
alors qu'on envoie un enfant
chercher sans confident
du lait dans la nuit.

SEPARATION

In a shed in the old garden
the separation takes place
amid the rustling of leaves
you have to go far away
to another country
to recover this moment of farewell
leaning on the quiet tree
in the hour of lamplight
just as a child is sent
with no one to confide in
looking for milk in the night.

TRAGIQUE DU TEMPS

La porte si forte des prisons
le vent passe dessous quand même
parfois aussi un pâle soleil
en un vieux temps nuance les plis
d'une robe de bourreau.
Dans un bourg de vacances
commence à jouer une harmonie
tandis qu'ayant posé sa houe
assis un journalier contemple
les exécutants pacifiques
voués au massacre
dans l'année
disant croire à leurs âmes éternelles
à leurs corps ressuscitant.

TRAGEDY OF THE TIME

The prison door so strong
but wind gets under it just the same
sometimes also a pale sunbeam
in an olden time
touches the folds of the hangman's cloak.
In a resort town
a band begins to play
while a day laborer
having put aside his hoe
sits contemplating
the peaceful performers
all to be massacred
within the year
claiming to believe in their eternal souls
and the resurrection of their bodies.

PRÉTEXTES

Pour partir
les prétextes abondent
réentendre un pas
le bruit d'un outil
revoir sources, abîmes
l'homme assis qui ne parle pas
la grille haute d'un jardin
d'où des cris s'élèvent
et qu'entourent des murs à tessons
se dressant sur le ciel
par temps d'orage.

PRETEXTS

The pretexts for leaving
are many
to hear a footstep again
or the noise of a hand tool
to see again springs and depths
the seated man who does not speak
the high iron palings of a garden
from which screams arise
surrounded by spiked walls
standing stark against the sky
in times of storm.

VOYAGE

Sous le soleil du soir
le pain sec
garde un goût de légende
la blessure survenue en écartant l'épine
rassérène une âme avivée
des hameaux se montrent aux tournants
des arbres font des signes
du monde en noir entre dans une maison
le voyageur du regard
suit des lignes d'ornières
des oiseaux criaillent
le zénith ne bouge où pointe une étoile.

JOURNEY

As the sun goes down
dry bread
keeps its taste of legend
the wound sustained in removing the thorn
calms a troubled soul
hamlets appear around bends
trees make signs
people in black enter a house
with his eyes the traveller
follows the ruts in the road
birds squawk
directly overhead where a star shines
nothing moves.

L'HABITUDE

Au bord de la table
celui-là qui fait jouer
la limaille et l'aimant
n'entend plus l'océan
battre les schistes.
Au plafond pendent
les haricots qui sèchent
les murs blancs de chaux
laissent aller leurs insectes
des gens qui se croisent
voudraient retrouver
l'habitude d'aimer.

HABIT

At the edge of the table
the man who is toying with
the magnet and filings
no longer hears the ocean
beating the rocks.
From the ceiling
beans are hung to dry
the whitewashed walls
let insects come and go
people passing each other by
would like to get back
in the habit of loving.

MORBUS

A ta santé morbus
clame à la porte de la guinguette
l'ivrogne épuisé.
Dans toutes les ruelles
on appelle une charrette
qui ramène les morts.
D'aucuns cherchent à croire
à aimer devant l'épouvante
un lapin blanc
grignote en sa cage pourrie
abandonné au temps.

CHOLERA

To your health cholera
shouts the exhausted drunk
at the tavern door.
In all the alleyways
they call for the cart
that carries away the dead.
Some seek faith
some seek love in the face of terror
a white rabbit
abandoned to the elements
gnaws at its decaying cage.

BOURGADE

Dans une bourgade à encoignures
un drapier se tient
sur le pas d'une porte
le trône vacille
déclare-t-il en regardant les nuages
des femmes, dont une en deuil
viennent acheter malgré la déroute de leur corps
un pain coutumier
à forme de collier de cheval
gémissant sur son prix qui monte.

TOWN

In a town of twisting streets
the clothier stands
on a doorstep
the throne is unsteady
he declares as he watches the clouds
women, one of them in mourning
come despite their bodily decline to buy
the usual bread
in the shape of a horse collar
groaning over its rising price.

LA BARRICADE

Seul il n'arrête pas de revoir
malgré les arbres verts
comme dessinée à l'encre de Chine
la barricade;
l'air fouette les visages aigris
près d'une cage à vieux oiseaux
ceux qui têtus sourient
à l'amour exigeant
écoutent sonner l'heure.
L'homme a senti
au café du matin
sa doublure usée
à l'endroit du cœur.

THE BARRICADE

Alone he can't stop seeing
despite the green trees
the barricade
as if drawn in India ink
sour faces are whipped by the wind
near a cage of old birds
those who smile obstinately
at love's demands
hear the stroke of the hour.
Over his morning coffee
the man felt
the lining worn
in the area of his heart.

CÉRÉMONIE

La cérémonie
commença avec une lenteur composée
mais le vin provoqua des colères inhumaines
un bouquet tomba d'un corsage
l'entame d'une brioche
le soir vira au sombre
des corps s'étreignirent sous les lampes
un souffle pur monta de la terre
des portraits impassibles
aux murs souriaient.
Prisonniers de leur matière exploitée
des objets d'autrefois
se brisèrent au grand jour
du lendemain sur la terre fertile.

CEREMONY

The ceremony
began with slow composure
but the wine provoked inhuman rages
a corsage fell from a blouse
the first slice from a cake
the evening turned dark
bodies clasped each other under the lamps
a pure breath rose from the earth
impassive portraits
smiled on the walls.
Prisoners of the matter that made them
things of the past
the next morning on the fertile earth
broke in broad daylight.

UNE ÉPOQUE

On entend le chant monotone
de l'ortolan
l'aire est nue
à l'époque de ceux
qui signent d'une croix.
Toutes les choses à dire
restent loin de l'être profond
l'avenir entier
demeure imperceptible
dans un monde investi
par le rêve sévère.

AN ERA

The bunting's monotonous song
is audible
the threshing floor is bare
in the era of those
who sign with an X.
All the things to say
remain far from deepest being
the entire future
remains unheard-of
in a world beset
by harsh dreams.

EMPIRE

Un mannequin absorbé par l'ombre
par terre un clou
le regard vide d'un empereur
au milieu des feuilles
près de chaumières terreuses
des lueurs s'accrochent à la blouse d'un assidu
aux jupes d'une songeuse
l'escalier est sans rampe
dans la venelle.
L'abattant du secrétaire porte des taches
hors de tout bruit
le soleil déjà haut au ciel.

EMPIRE

A mannequin immersed in shadow
a nail on the ground
an emperor's blank gaze
in the midst of the leaves
near huts of thatch and mud
sheens catch on the workingman's shirt
on the skirts of a woman who dreams
there is no handrail on the stairs
in the alley.
The desk top is stained
beyond all sound
the sun is already high in the sky.

TRANSFIGURATION

Une rousse chevelure
demeure intacte
sur la tête de mort féminine exhumée.
Dans le champ emmuré
des racines sortent d'une terre avide.
D'un coup dans une vie
la gaieté se brise
comme un piège.
Le même jour à des hommes
le Christ apparaît pour tout
transfigurer.

TRANSFIGURATION

A head of red hair
remains intact
on the exhumed woman's skull.
In the field enclosed by walls
roots emerge from a greedy earth.
All at once in a life
joy snaps
like a trap.
The same day
Christ appears to some men
to transfigure all.

CES TROIS POMMES DERNIÈRES

Un homme dit dans la boutique
ces trois pommes dernières
je les prends
on les lui pèse et vend.
Une femme qui les eût voulues dit :
il y a toujours quelqu'un pour acheter ce qui reste
or le pâle acquéreur
qui connaissait peu d'étreintes amoureuses
ce soir tenant les fruits en main
s'en fut droit vers sa mort.

THESE LAST THREE APPLES

In a shop a man says
these last three apples
I'll take them
they are weighed and sold to him.
A woman who would have wanted to get them says:
there is always someone to buy what's left
whereupon the pale purchaser
who knew little of love's embraces
went that evening with the fruit in hand
straight to his death.

C'EST LA VIE

Dans la pièce au sol en terre
une mouche monte au long
d'une draperie usée.
En confiance chantent des femmes
elles conservent sur le tard
un rire de fraîcheur
leur corps entier qui fut beau
de sang s'irrigue et dure.
Cessant tout bruit, se regardant
c'est la vie
pensent-elles.

THAT'S LIFE

In the room with the dirt floor
a fly climbs the length
of a worn drape.
Women are confidently singing
late in the day they still have
fresh laughter
their bodies which once were beautiful
keep pumping blood and endure.
Stopping all the noise
looking at each other
they think
that's life.

TRANSLATOR'S NOTES

Pleasures Taken in Reading, Liberties in Rendering

Title

Much of Jean Follain's skill as a poet lies in his use of ambiguity. It is one of the sorrows of translation not to be able to render all the richnesses of meaning. Trying to translate the title of this collection posed a characteristic problem: How to preserve the reference to time embedded in the title while not misrepresenting the primary meaning? "After All" is less than faithful; "According to Everything" is wrong in tone and music. I wanted to communicate to English readers Follain's turning of "*d'après*," which usually precedes a literary reference, toward the evidences of the world ("*tout*") rather than back to a written tradition. In the end, encouraged by a friend, the poet Robert Hass, I decided not to do any of the English violences to the title but to offer the book under its most suggestive name—the French one.

Table of Contents

Even a list of titles can be good reading, if the writer is Follain. Here the sequences suggest relations of space and time that anticipate the concerns of the poems themselves. See, for example, how the poem "The Wheel" is followed by "Wonders of the Circle," and this in turn by "Hoops." Or

179

how "The Beautiful Day" is followed by "A Single Day" and later "Twilight" and the poem of night "So Light."

The Poems

SYMBOLS OF TIME

The literal translation of the first line, "In this universe of flight they go," *sounds* translated in English. It seemed to me that the sense of the line was to locate us in a world where taking flight had become part of the nature of things, so I translated it with a more natural expression in English.

THE ART OF WAR

"*Taupe*" means "mole," the animal. But in English the word "mole," occurring as it would after the second line's "nipple," would provoke an erroneous association. Therefore I took the liberty of referring simply to an animal that burrows; the trenches and the grave are still implied, the significant ironies unmarred by a bad pun. See my note on "By the Same Tree" for a similar instance.

TIED SHOE

"*Paresse de vivre*" in the penultimate line might be read as an ironic play on the expression "*joie de vivre.*"

IT'S NOT ALL SAID

Translating the title of this poem posed another special problem. On the one hand, it means "not everything is spoken"—that is, there are things before and beyond the capacities of language. On the other hand, perhaps even more immediately, it means "all is not (yet) said (and done)," or, there is more to come of language, and this is not the last word. Both of these meanings are available to readers of the French; they remind us, after the hints of Eden in the poem, of the first sentence of the book of Genesis.

INHABITED INTERIOR

In the original, beauty is at once a woman (the mother? the wife?) and a quality or ideal. The beauty is *in* the house; the space is inhabited; the body has a soul. In this case, the loveliness of the remembered home is a kind of female *genius loci.*

THE SEARCH

This provides a good example of the way Follain expresses intellectual or emotional states through objects in the poem. Here things with uncertain footings seem to become emblems of an ontological insecurity: What are the grounds and bases for our lives? The stem of the glass breaks, the girl has lost her slipper, and the whole house, we eventually see, is founded on the edge of an abyss. This kind of telescoping (in which the scene is first viewed in intimate particularity and then gradually from farther and farther away, until we see the building around the human figure, the continent around the building, the universe around the planet) is one of Follain's characteristic gestures. See also "Man Alone," "Protected," "Work," "Journey," "These Last Three Apples." Moving through imagination toward the micro- or macrocosmic, Follain places human perceptions and values in a perspective that shakes us a little from our anthropocentricity.

WORK

Note how Follain's attention to the insect climbing the table makes more flexible our sense of dimension: later, when the workshop is called "giant," we are able to accept it partly because we have been reminded of another organism's perceptual scale. In the end, then, when the studio is seen to be posed on the edge of a cliff, it is as if we are assuming the vantage point of some much larger-than-human observer. In the poem "Protected," Follain's relativistic slant becomes quite explicit ("a space-time curve"). Everywhere the scientist in him is at work: a judicious eye, clinical dispassion, predilection for a spare, descriptive language punctuated now and then by rarer or more academic words (see "Hecatomb," for example, or the word "*litharge*," or oxidized lead, in "*Retour ou Pas*").

THE REAL CHILD

"*Temps mort*" means "idle time." This seems intimately related to the English colloquialism "to kill time," and since I wanted to preserve the hint of death embedded in these terms, I took advantage of the coincidence.

TIMES

"*Terre argileuse*" I have rendered simply as "clay," because the corresponding adjectival forms in English are so clumsy (clayey, clayish, claylike) and because none of the intimations of mortality is lost in the abbreviation.

SOLITARY INKWELL

The common name for a mushroom heads this poem allowing it, figuratively, to be read as an account of the act of poetry itself, moving from solitude to community through its audiences, altering their experience of the world. Compare "Wonders of the Circle" for another account of the magical (almost hallucinogenic) powers of language.

BY THE SAME TREE

The word "bark," followed so soon by the word "dog," results in a pun in English that would not be present in the original and that radically detracts from the subtler powers of the ending. I have therefore substituted "trunk."

SEASON

Note how etymology informs the use of the word "robust": the first three lines remind us that strength may reside not only in fixed footings, since the sturdiness of robust has its roots in the Latin word for oak. "Toward the horizon that opens" too clumsily appends expansiveness to the end of the sentence in the literal translation of the last line. The sense, it seemed to me, was that these two didn't have to run or hide and that the horizon that opens might simply be where the woods end.

ANIMATION

I had great difficulty understanding the line "*au jour à l'autre attentives*," and Madame Follain herself couldn't make sense of it, suggesting that I suppress it. Instead I've approximated the meaning as best I can from its context, rather than tear the fabric of connections and timing in the poem. I trust that readers will consult the French to form their own conclusions.

My reading of the poem plays the representation of the real against the representation of the representation. That is, the poem became for me an expression of the living power of a work of art in an ambience of idleness, senselessness, indulgence. In the translation, the word "still" should work to suggest both persistence in time and motionlessness in space, in this *nature morte* of a faintly prerevolutionary garden, its inviolate calm about to turn illusory. Suddenly in the painting what happens is actual—a riot of color, an insurgent mob, the frame itself almost a doorway or window. Responsibility begins in response, and the power of art here is politically active.

THE LOCKERT LIBRARY OF POETRY
IN TRANSLATION

George Seferis: Collected Poems (1924-1955), translated, edited, and introduced by Edmund Keeley and Philip Sherrard

Collected Poems of Lucio Piccolo, translated and edited by Brian Swann and Ruth Feldman

C.P. Cavafy: Collected Poems, translated by Edmund Keeley and Philip Sherrard and edited by George Savidis

Benny Andersen: Selected Poems, translated by Alexander Taylor

Selected Poetry of Andrea Zanzotto, translated and edited by Ruth Feldman and Brian Swann

Poems of René Char, translated by Mary Ann Caws and Jonathan Griffin

Selected Poems of Tudor Arghezi, translated and edited by Michael Impey and Brian Swann

Tadeus Różewicz: The Survivor, translated and introduced by Magnus J. Krynski and Robert A. Maguire

"Harsh World" and Other Poems by Ángel González, translated by Donald D. Walsh

Dante's "Rime," translated and introduced by Patrick S. Diehl

Ritsos in Parentheses, translations and introduction by Edmund Keeley

Salamander: Selected Poems of Robert Marteau, translated and introduced by Anne Winters

Angelos Sikelianos: Selected Poems, translated and introduced by Edmund Keeley and Philip Sherrard

The Dawn is Always New: Selected Poetry of Rocco Scotellaro, translated by Ruth Feldman and Brian Swann

Selected Later Poems of Marie Luise Kaschnitz, translated by Lisel Mueller

Osip Mandelstam's "Stone," translated and introduced by Robert Tracy

The Man I Pretend to Be: "The Colloquies" and Selected Poems of Guido Gozzano, translated and edited by Michael Palma, with an introductory essay by Eugenio Montale

Sounds, Feelings, Thoughts: Seventy Poems by Wistawa Szymborska, translated by Magnus J. Krynski and Robert A. Maguire

D'Après Tout: Poems by Jean Follain, translated by Heather McHugh

Library of Congress Cataloging in Publication Data

Follain, Jean, 1903-1971.
    D'après tout.

    (Lockert library of poetry in translation)
    I.   McHugh, Heather, 1948-   II.   Title.
III.   Series.
PQ2611.0612D313   1981   841'.912   81-47126
ISBN 0-691-06476-8   AACR2
ISBN 0-691-01372-1 (pbk.)